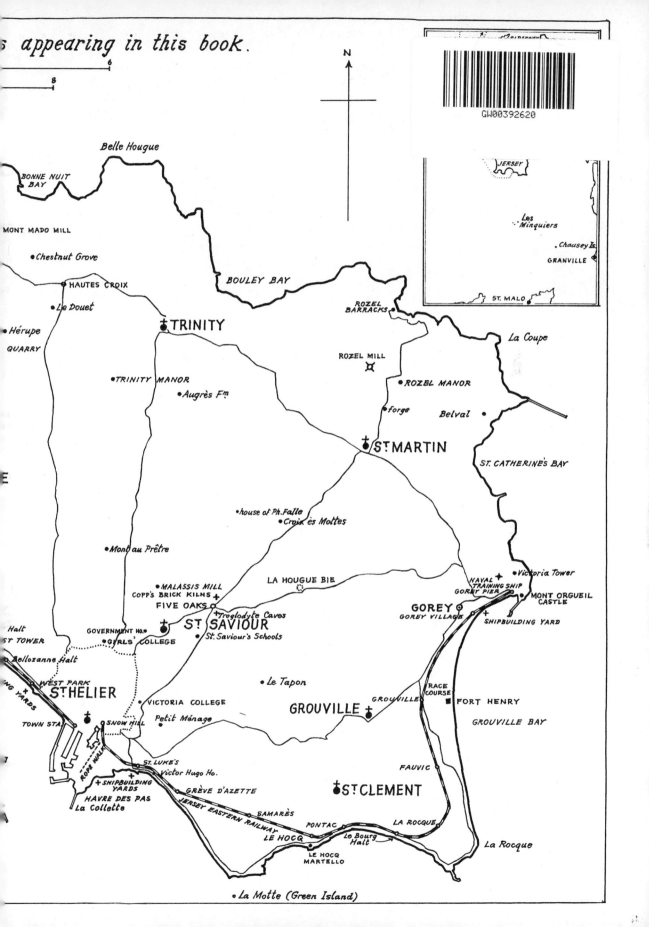

appearing in this book.

N

GW00392620

Belle Hougue

BONNE NUIT
BAY

MONT MADO MILL

Chestnut Grove

BOULEY BAY

HAUTES CROIX

Le Douet

Hérupe
QUARRY

†TRINITY

ROZEL
BARRACKS

La Coupe

ROZEL MILL

TRINITY MANOR

Augrès Fm

ROZEL MANOR

forge   Belval

†St MARTIN

ST. CATHERINE'S BAY

house of Ph.Falle

Croix ès Mottes

Mont au Prêtre

LA HOGUE BIE

MALASSIS MILL

COPP'S BRICK KILNS

FIVE OAKS

Troglodyte Caves

†St SAVIOUR

Victoria Tower

NAVAL
TRAINING SHIP
GOREY PIER

GOREY

MONT ORGUEIL
CASTLE

GOREY VILLAGE

SHIPBUILDING YARD

GOVERNMENT HO.

GIRLS' COLLEGE

St.Saviour's Schools

Halt
ST TOWER

Bellozanne Halt

Le Tapon

RACE
COURSE

GROUVILLE

FORT HENRY

WEST PARK

St HELIER

Victoria College

GROUVILLE

TOWN STA.

SNOW HILL

Petit Ménage

GROUVILLE BAY

ST. LUKE'S

Victor Hugo Ho.

FAUVIC

†St CLEMENT

SHIPBUILDING
YARDS

GRÈVE D'AZETTE

HAVRE DES PAS

La Collette

JERSEY EASTERN RAILWAY

SAMARÈS

LA ROCQUE

PONTAC

LA ROCQUE

La Rocque

LE HOCQ

Le Bourg
Halt

LE HOCQ
MARTELLO

La Motte (Green Island)

JERSEY

Les
Minquiers

Chausey Is.
GRANVILLE

ST. MALO

JERSEY THROUGH THE LENS

1. Le Hocq Tower, a late 18th century coastal defence, commonly called a Martello Tower. In the foreground a farmer makes up his load of vraic. *c.* 1914.

JERSEY
through the lens

Photographs taken before 1918

compiled by

RICHARD MAYNE and **JOAN STEVENS**

of La Société Jersiaise

PHILLIMORE

1975

Published by
PHILLIMORE & CO. LTD.
London and Chichester

Head Office: Shopwyke Hall,
Chichester, Sussex, England.

© La Société Jersiaise, 1975

ISBN   0   85033   211   7

Printed and bound in Great Britain by
BILLING & SONS LIMITED

Dedicated to all the early Jersey photographers
and particularly to

EMILE F. GUITON, 1879-1972

*Secretary, Curator and Membre d'Honneur of La Société Jersiaise,
who, as an amateur, photographed Jersey for us throughout his life*

ACKNOWLEDGEMENTS

La Société Jersiaise is much indebted to those who have assisted in the compilation of this book.

The majority of the photographs shown are drawn from our own large and comprehensive collection, but the following have been lent to us for reproduction, the owners retaining copyright.

Mrs. P. Armstrong	..	34, 174
Mr. J. O. Arthur	..	39, 40, 66
Mr. C. Bisson ..	..	9
Mr. F. Buesnel ..	..	37
Mr. E. G. Copp	..	160, 161
Mr. R. De Faye	..	156
Mr. S. Gavey ..	..	27, 28, 67, 158, 159
Mr. E. R. Le Conte	..	94
Mrs. T. Marett ..	..	162
Mr. R. Mayne ..	..	17, 18, 25, 32, 57, 64, 80, 84, 85, 86, 92, 131, 134, 143, 147, 148, 149, 153, 163, 165, 166
Miss B. Mourant	..	50
Mrs. G. Moutant	..	88, 153, 154
Mr. P. Ozouf ..	..	24
Mrs. A. Renouf	..	10, 72, 125
Mrs. J. Stevens ..	..	38, 132
Mrs. D. Wallbridge	..	23

We are most grateful to all those who have been willing to let us see their collections, and choose from amongst them.

Some of our helpers deserve a special mention. Mrs. Wallbridge has been untiring in finding rare photographs, and collecting information about them, and assisting us to identify people shown in groups. Mr. René Le Vaillant has expended much time and skill in copying photographs so that they could be reproduced, whether the negative was available or not, and usually it was not. Mr. H. Perrée has given us valuable information on agricultural matters, Mr. A. Brandon-Langley identified for us the medals shown in No. 48, and Mr. C. G. Stevens has drawn the end-paper maps. Mrs. W. Macready, the Honorary Secretary, and Mr. G. Drew, the Senior Attendant at the Museum, have always been ready to help.

For authorities we have drawn on the numerous articles in the *Bulletins of La Société Jersiaise,* and some books written by members of that Society.

CONTENTS

End-papers:　*front* The Town of St. Helier

back The Island of Jersey

LIST OF ILLUSTRATIONS

INTRODUCTION

In recent years various books have appeared in England portraying life a century ago, through the medium of early photographs.

We felt that Jersey must never lag behind, and knowing what a wealth of photographs there are at the Museum of La Société Jersiaise, we knew that our task would not be to find suitable material, but to make a selection from the rich store available. Inevitably some aspects of island life were not represented, and so we have gone to some private collections in order to cover the widest possible range of activities.

We have chosen a period from the earliest examples up to 1918, a coverage of about 60 years. Naturally some examples are faded, and have not reproduced very well, but we are sure that readers will recognise that we have, on occasion, included a picture for its historical significance in spite of its condition.

Many of these pictures are not dated, and where no date is available we have suggested one. What strikes one in endeavouring to do this, is how little life has changed during the period, and how much it has changed since, and often a photograph of 1890 could almost as well have been taken in 1910.

In making our selection we have tried to choose scenes which are typically Jersey, and could not be mistaken for England or France, or indeed Guernsey, and to show aspects of life peculiar to the Island, such as black butter making and vraicing. Unfortunately, many occupations which would have made fascinating pictures were not deemed worthy of photography. It is clear that the subjects most dear to our early photographers were portraiture and scenery, subjects of lesser interest for the purposes of a book such as this; if a time of day were carefully chosen to avoid all traffic, a study of La Corbière lighthouse would look no different to-day from one in 1874, when it was built, and so would not make a telling illustration. Indeed it is the motor car which bedevils photography now; if one could ever succeed in taking a town scene, for instance, without cars interrupting the composition, it would have to be done at dawn, when there would be no human activity to bring the picture to life, and it is people at work and play that we are endeavouring to show. How fortunate were our ancestors who could always catch a satisfactory and lively composition without a traffic menace.

We have found but few photographs which we can with confidence date before 1860, but this is hardly surprising in such a small and remote

1

island, although, as the list at the end of this book will show, some photographers were established here far earlier. Once in operation photographers multiplied, and some of the albums of portraiture at the Museum testify how people rushed to take advantage of this new and exciting invention, and new it would have seemed in 1860. Albert Smith was one of the many, and it is to him that we owe many of the pictures shown in this book.

It is the aim of this book to portray Jersey as it was about a century ago. What was important then was agriculture, defence, and sea-links with the mainland. The times have changed and the accent to-day falls on other activities, and it is this changing pattern of life which makes the early photographic records so valuable.

During the period reviewed links with England were becoming closer. This was partly due to steam replacing sail, making it feasible for islanders to visit the mainland, for work, commerce, or pleasure, and to send their children there for education, where Protestant influence would be assured, for the Jerseyman was a firm Anglican or Nonconformist. Again, the shipping industry with Canada and Newfoundland was conducted through English ports. The official lauguage of the Island remained French, and Jersey-French continued to be spoken and understood by most people, but the English language was gaining ground in schools, shops and socially, as is testified by diaries and letters of the period.

The strongest Anglicising influence, however, was the impact of the Napoleonic wars, which engendered strong anti-French feelings. Numbers of retired army and navy officers, with their families, migrated to Jersey after Waterloo, and later, and fine terraces of houses sprang up on the outskirts of the town to meet their needs. They found the Island congenial, temperate in climate, and economical in taxes, for living costs, and for the education of their children. At the same time, large numbers of workers, principally Irish, came over for the oyster fisheries and the building of St. Catherine's breakwater.

By the time photography became available, all these influences were established. Jersey retained its continental flavour, welcomed by those who had spent many years abroad in the Services, whilst remaining a part of the Crown domains, and in no way a foreign country.

Then a new industry evolved: tourism is the modern word. As soon as transport in the brave little mail steamers became available, people from Britain started to come to these islands for holidays, and to enjoy the sunshine and beaches, and to have the sensation of going abroad without actually leaving the British Isles. To serve this new influx, hotels and boarding houses sprang up, horse-drawn charabancs and coach tours were organised, and the shops increased their ranges and efficiency. All these aspects of life we have endeavoured to cover.

Architecture had, at this time, become the same as would be found in English towns, but for the preponderance of granite as a building material. However, to give the feeling, the very colour of Jersey, we have chosen to start this survey with a few early photographs of vernacular architecture, houses which have grown out of the living rock, our typical rosy-hued granite. And because producers are becoming increasingly important in a consumer world, we have chosen to start our survey with agriculture. Through the centuries it has been the fruits of the earth, and the men who produced them, who have been the mainstay of the population.

It is our hope that this book of photographs will bring pleasure to visitors who come to our Island from all over the world, and also to Jersey people, whether they live here, or whether they have gone afar, but retain, as Jerseymen always do, an affection for their Island home.

PART I – AGRICULTURE

Since Neolithic man first discovered the value of grain, his descendants have grown, ground and cooked it for their sustenance. So Jerseymen grew wheat, oats, barley and rye, and the importance they attached to the value of wheat is evinced by the large number of wind and water mills which existed, and the fact that legal transactions were conducted by payment in 'froment', that is, wheat. Parish taxes are still assessed so in name, though no longer in fact, a person's rateable value being stated in quarters (28lbs.) of wheat.

Some interesting ancient customs still survive, amongst them the 'branchage'. Once a year (it is twice annually now) the parish officials inspect the roads and see that they are kept clear for passing vehicles. It is the duty of every landowner to attend to his branchage, that is to cut back growth in hedge or bank, and to cut all over-hanging branches to a certain requisite height (12ft. on main roads and 10ft. on lesser roads). In origin this was to allow the free passage of vans loaded with hay or straw; all infringements are fined by the Constable of the parish and his officials. Each year the Royal Court officers make a ceremonial visit, the Visite Royale, to two of the 12 parishes, and proceed on foot down a selected route, the 'arpenteur' (assessor) measuring any suspected tree or branch. It is a parish group of St. Saviour, on such an occasion, which we illustrate, showing the rector, the Reverend E. Luce, a well-known and popular figure. At that period the parish rectors still had seats in the States Assembly.

Another custom is the collection of 'bannelais', or road sweepings. The manner of disposing of them varies between parishes, but usually they are swept into small heaps, and the proprietor of the adjoining land thus has some good fertiliser, for they were then composed of horse manure and leaves.

Wheat and oats were usually cut in August (hence 'aouster', meaning to reap) and made into corn stacks, later to be threshed by communal threshing machines which visited the larger farms. Threshing day was a great occasion when neighbours brought their corn to a central farm, and all worked together on a co-operative basis. The first threshing machine known in Jersey appeared in about 1860. Much cider was consumed, and needed, for such hot and dusty work.

Cider making was a most important industry and export. In 1800 it was estimated that about 15 per cent. of all arable land was under apple orchards, and two million gallons of cider were produced annually, much of it exported. Jersey has never made beer or wine on any great scale, so that cider was the main drink for everyone. The apples were picked in the autumn, and heaped in piles in the orchards, the different varieties being carefully chosen and blended. In due course they were crushed in the circular granite trough, 'le tou', by the action of the stone wheel, 'la meule', pulled by a horse. The pulp, 'le mar', was then spread on sacking or layers of wheat straw, and pressed in the 'prinseu', the juice flowing out into barrels for later fermentation. A side produce of the cider industry was black butter, 'le nier beurre', a conserve made of apples, sugar, spices and cider, and cooked for 24 hours, this being an occasion for communal activity and much merriment. Many delicious local dishes contain apples as a main ingredient.

The origin of the Jersey cow is not known with certainty, but she probably came here from France, and perhaps from much further south. However, her present excellence is the result of careful breeding and culling since the middle of the last century. Indeed since 1789 (with the exception of slaughter animals during the years of the Second World War) no live bovine has been allowed into the Island, so that the strain has remained pure for almost two centuries. Her characteristics are smallness, gentleness, and the richness of her milk. She has a straight back and a well-formed udder and finely modelled head with a charming dish face; her large dark eyes and long black eyelashes make her the envy of every beauty queen. The most usual colour is a pale biscuit, but it can vary from off-white to almost black, a shade known as mulberry.

Deep ploughing used to be done with the implement drawn by six horses, this again being a communal effort; since the beginning of this century all ploughs have been metal, and the two animals nearest the plough were the strongest and were said to be 'au câgnon'. Four men with spades were needed to dig the corners, the 'piquage' and 'dépiquage', and others might be needed to straighten out here and there. In the days when farmers had only light wooden five-tine scarifiers they had difficulty in breaking down old turf, and the breaking up of large clods of grass was called 'rabillage'. 'Le dîner d'la grande tchéthue' (the Big Plough Dinner) was the generous and delicious dinner served by the wife of the host farmer where the big plough was operating, consisting of an allowance of one pound of beef per man, with potatoes and apple pie.

Potatoes have been grown in Jersey for a long time, but they have become increasingly important since about 1870. Efforts to catch the high prices of the early market in England have resulted in the crop being dug before it is really mature, thus producing about half the export tonnage there used to be. Planting took place in February and March, and digging in May and June, and was done by a team, usually Bretons, who came over for the season. The group of three persons was composed of 'la frouque', the digger, 'l'élopeur', the shaker, and 'le glianeur' (or 'la glianeuse'), the picker, who was most often a woman. The man in charge of one or more groups working on the farm was called 'le tâcheron'.

The potatoes were sorted into wares and mids, and put into barrels accordingly. They were then loaded on to the van and taken to town, where the farmer had them weighed at the central weighbridges near the harbour, and around which a constant form of buying or auction was taking place, causing a most animated scene. Having taken his load to the store of the merchant who had bought it, he then returned to the weighbridge to weigh his empty van, then to wend his way home with barrels and a weary horse. Both skill and fun went into choosing when and to whom to sell, as news of the current price passed like wildfire down the waiting queues of vans, sometimes stretching back almost as far as First Tower. The homing farmer would give his friends who were still waiting their turn the latest news of prices offered. Queues from the western parishes came along the Esplanade, those from the north came down New Street, and those from the east through the town. This was a facet of local life which has quite disappeared, and which, though anxious and very hard work, was most exciting. Anyone who took part in it cannot forget the thrill of anticipation if the news was good, and there was a chance of returning home having got a better price than one had expected.

Vraic, or seaweed, has from the earliest times been esteemed as a fertiliser, particularly on light soil, and its collection on the beaches used to be a great event in the farming calendar, controlled by law and usage. When and where any man could collect his vraic was well known and strictly adhered to, and after high spring tides the beaches swarmed with carts, all there to collect this priceless, but free, gift from nature. This vraic, and the ashes of burnt dried vraic, had long been found to be the best natural replacement for the lack of chalk and lime in the soil of the Island.

The culture of tomatoes was at its zenith between the wars, but had started somewhat earlier. They were planted straight into the ground the very day that the potatoes were lifted, and they grew particularly well in the light soil of the southern parishes.

The pattern of agriculture has naturally changed over the years, and new crops are tried, and either continued or discarded, according to their success and the prevailing economic factors. With labour costs and freight charges on exports, farmers face serious problems, but the appearance of Jersey, if it is to retain its character, must remain rural.

2. The Old Poingdestre farm at Mont au Prêtre. The entrance is dated 1660, and the pillars were a later alteration to a traditional entrance. Note the thatch universal in the country, but never seen now. *c.* 1910.

3. The paved farmyard, 'Le Bel'. Note the stone trough beside the well.

4. The pedestrian arch at Morel Farm, dated 1666. This fine property is owned by the National Trust for Jersey.

5.   L'Ancienneté at St. Brelade in about 1900.

6.   The same house some years later. Stone features from L'Ancienneté were incorporated in the rebuilding of Trinity Manor in 1910.

7.   The birthplace of the Reverend Philippe Falle, 1656-1742, historian, and founder of Jersey's public library in 1737. This house, in St. Saviour, was demolished in 1904. The library building has been preserved.

8. A steam threshing machine. The carts on the left have brought barrels of water to cool the engine, which has no binding device, and consequently many men were needed to bundle the straw. It was then passed to the next man who forked it up to the loft. One small bundle has been put in front of the cart, for show. *c.* 1910.

9. The collection of 'bannelais', road sweepings, used as a fertiliser. The farmer is Mr. J. E. Vautier with his son. *c.* 1905.

10.   Oats being stacked in August, for threshing by a communal thresher later. At the Renouf farm at Sorel.

11.   Cornstacks at Valley Farm, St. Mary. Gigoulande, the only double wheeled Mill in the Island, has been demolished, but the mill buildings can be seen on the left.

12. A farmer lifts his crop of seed potatoes, to be stored for next year's planting. The enormous crop is noteworthy and also the large number of labourers employed, as also the traditional type of potato box in which seed is kept. In the autumn these tubers are 'stood', that is packed neatly in the boxes, with the 'eye' upwards. From this the shoot grows, so that when the seed is planted in the spring, it already has a strong and healthy shoot an inch or so high.

13.   Cider making at Les Augres Trinity. The apples were crushed in the circular stone trough by the action of the stone wheel. Cider crushers are usually made of Chausey granite and are composed of eight, or more, curved sections.

14.   A cider crusher in a barn, the more usual position. Note the 'grappin' and rakes stored above it. Being in use only seasonally, it has accumulated some rubbish in the centre.

15. (*above*)   A cider press. The stone crusher is often wrongly called the press.

16. (*left*)   Another type of press The apple pulp is separated by layers of straw. Note that the barrel which receives the juice is sunk into the ground. Usually it was in a pit below the press.

17. Barrels of apple pulp, before being pressed. This is probably at Le Douet, St. John, where cider was produced on a commercial scale.

18. Black butter making in 1915. The cauldron 'un peile' is standing on a 'trepid'. The butter is constantly stirred with long handled wooden spoons.

16

19. Milking at Broadfields, St. Lawrence, a Gibaut property. This was a dairy collecting centre, where butter was made, hence the big churn on the left, which is an unusual type for Jersey.

20. It used to be common practice to milk in the field. Note the milkman's three-legged stool, and the typical Jersey milk can covered with a filter cloth.

21.   A posed photograph of a family with their workers and herd. Potatoes are being dug, and the horse has been un-harnessed from the van, loaded with cental (100lbs.) barrels. Father has been milking, the daughter fondles her favourite cow, and Grannie has taken refreshments to the field.

22.   'La Grande Tchéthue', the Big Plough. The two strongest horses are put nearest the plough. This must be in about 1900, as the plough is metal.

23. A potato digging group, with the family and workers of Mr. J. Le Conte of Three Oaks Farm, St. Lawrence. The barrels are finished off with the 'toppers' the biggest specimens.

24. 'The Last Load'. A posed photograph of the Ozouf family and their workers at Le Tapon Farm, St. Saviour, in 1918. The 4 cabot potato barrels, ready for export, are packed with straw and covered with willow tops and are ready to go to town, as the workers bring out boxes of tomato seedlings, with cans of water. In empty barrels may be seen tomato canes, and the man on the right holds a hammer, ready to knock them into the ground beside each tomato plant, the soil usually being very dry at the time. Everyone in the family is enjoying this big moment when one crop gives way to the next.

25. Breton labourers in French Lane (Hilgrove Street) at Le Soleil Levant. Note that the women from the different regions wear distinctive head dresses and shawls. *c.* 1900.

26. A group of parochial officals in about 1890, on their annual Visite du Branchage. Left to right, **Top Row:** Driver, Mr. F. J. Bois, ?, Mr. C. Mourant, Mr. John Buesnel, Mr. P. B. Sauvage, ?, Centenier P. V. Cooke, Mr. J. J. Romeril. **Middle Row:** Mr. P. Le S. Mourant (Bram Bilo), ?, Cabot, Road Inspector Mr. T. P. Laurens (Parish Hall), Mr. J. F. Le Rendu, Mr. C. Le Boutillier. **Bottom Row:** ?, Mr. J. J. Ereaut, Rev. E. Luce, Mr. J. H. L'Amy, Mr. J. Buesnel.

27.   Mr. T. Hotton, of St. John, with a load of potatoes in sacks, for export to the Army in 1917, hence the broad arrows marked on the sacks. The typical local van existed in the Island from about 1875, and was a spring vehicle serving many purposes. This is the five-panel type and could take a load of two tons, or more with a second horse. This van cost £50 and was built by Colbacks of Trinity.

28.   An early mechanical digger 'The Jersey Lily' in use from about 1900. It was heavy to pull and needed two horses. The photograph shows Mr. and Mrs. Hotton, of Chestnut Grove, St. John, and in the background, Mr. S. Gavey. The horses are Bob and Brown.

29.   Vraic carts, making up their loads from the prepared piles of vraic (seaweed) on the right. Each cart has two horses, indicating that the homeward journey will be uphill.

30.   Gathering vraic at Le Pulec, St. Ouen, one of the richest areas for finding this priceless fertiliser. Note the carts have slatted sides, to allow the water to drain.

31. Jersey cabbages, or Long Jacks (*brassica oleracea longata*). This plant was used principally for animal feeding, and the stalks were made into walking sticks. Their culture has almost ceased. *c.* 1900.

32. Tomatoes being packed for export. The fruit was brought to the merchant in special trays (*see left*) similar to but not exactly the same as the potato box. It was then packed in plywood baskets for export. *c.* 1913.

33. Mal Assis Mill (now demolished) in the severe winter of 1895, when eighteen days of snow were recorded, unprecedented in Jersey.

34. The windmill at Bel Royal in 1860. Of the buildings shown in this photograph only the house on the left remains. The tower was blown up by the Germans at the beginning of the war. It was referred to as a Martello Tower in 1847, the earliest recorded use of the name in Jersey. The long building between the mill and the tower was Baxter's Steam Mill.

35.   The windmill at Mont Mado, built before 1830, and demolished early in this century. This photograph was taken before 1879, and the owner of the covered cart seems to have brought his family for a picnic. It has been suggested that he was a doctor ministering to the workers in the quarry below the mill.

36.   The windmill at Rosel in about 1880. Note the tail rod is secured to a cartwheel.

37.   A field of swedes being pulled, and arranged in neat rows, to be collected in the ubiquitous box cart. The owner here is Mr. E. G. Buesnel, of Bel Val, St. Martin, and his initials EGBN can be seen on the horse covers.

38.   A farm group, at Hérupe Farm, St. John, 1897. The family are, left to right: Elie Josué Simon, Francois Jean Simon (brother) in the carriage with Fanny and Starlight. A French manservant, Betsy Simon, Julie Simon (*née* Bisson), Mary Jane Sarre, (wife of E. J. Simon), Lydia Susan Simon, Anne Henriette Galdoé, Julia Anne Simon, (aged 4), Charles Simon sen., and Charles Simon jun., with Gay Lord the bull. The long granite bench was known as 'Mr. Nicolle's sofa' because a former owner, Mr. Nicolle, used to take a daily nap there after dinner.

39.   A young Jersey bull. Photograph by Godfray, therefore before 1900.

40.   A Jersey cow. Her mistress is wearing a traditional sunbonnet. By modern standards the cow's back would not be sufficiently straight, but otherwise she is a fine animal.

PART II – MILITARY MATTERS

Most writers are agreed that the Jersey Militia originates from 1337, when the Guardian of the Islands (at that time only one Guardian or Warden was appointed for the Channel Islands group), Thomas Ferrers, was ordered by the King to levy all able-bodied men, and to employ them for the defence of the Islands. However, there is evidence that local men had been called upon to defend their native land earlier still. By the 16th century this militia was organised into 'trained bands', one for each of the 12 parishes. By the next century these bands had been formed into three regiments, West, North and East, and a troop of horse was added later with 24 field pieces. Arms and equipment were provided by the British Government. By the next century five regiments had evolved, serving respectively, the N.W., N.E., S.E., S.W., and the Town with St. Lawrence.

The artillery guns were kept in the parish churches, but the troops had nowhere to drill, or to receive instruction in bad weather, and nowhere to store their armaments. Sir John Le Couteur, a famous Jerseyman, was devoting his energy to this matter in 1829, and drill sheds were then constructed for each parish, always near the parish church.

The arsenals were begun in 1835 for the proper storage of equipment; there were six of them, St. Mary, St. Peter, St. Lawrence, St. Martin, Grouville, and St. Helier: they were fine granite buildings and extremely good examples of the architecture of the period.

It is impossible to be concise about militia matters, as the situation changed so many times over the years, as new Militia Laws came into being, according to the needs of the times and the political climate of opinion. In general, though, all fit men between the ages of 17 and 65 had to serve, and it was General Le Couteur, the father of Sir John, who instituted boys' drill, for those under 17, when he was Adjutant-General from 1800-1811.

In all the attacks on the Island the Jersey Militia has played a conspicuous rôle, particularly in the case of the Battle of Jersey in 1781. Coastal watch, or 'guet' was a vital part of the militiaman's work, and the shores were (and are) ringed with defence works of all dates. In 1814 General Sir Hilgrove Turner expressed the view that the militia was 'an establishment superior to any of that nature existing in Europe'. Regular army instructors were attached to the units, but the officers, with the exception sometimes of the Adjutant, were all volunteers.

In 1831 William IV accorded to the Jersey Militia the prefix 'Royal', in recognition of the part they had played 50 years previously at the Battle of Jersey.

In 1877, a period when some of our photographs were taken, the Militia was again reorganised, this time into three Infantry Regiments, each of 500 men: they comprised the 1st (West and South), the 2nd (North and East), and the 3rd (Town). (Note that the term 'Town' is always used in militia contexts, and not St. Helier, which is surprising.) At the same time the Artillery was re-formed with four Batteries and 280 men. In 1881 Queen Victoria awarded 'Jersey 1781' as a battle honour to be blazoned on the Colour of each regiment.

Service in the Militia was a highlight in the lives of many men, and in 'Jèrri jadis', Mr. George Le Feuvre has given a vivid picture of his memories of the time when he was a recruit at the age of sixteen. He tells us: 'There was not a man in the world prouder than I the first time I put on my uniform to go to the camp at Quennevais with my rifle on my shoulder. It seemed to me that I was as handsome as any regular soldier, and I would have given anything to have met one of my girl friends that morning'. He was proud to find that his military number was 1781, recalling the famous battle. He records the camaraderie, the fun, and the good food, and the firm but kind understanding of the officers, who knew 'that most militiamen were more used to handling a plough than a rifle'. Church parade was preceded, on the Saturday evening, by much cleaning and polishing of uniforms for the great occasion. The regiment would march to church, headed by its band, and all the people came out of their houses to see them pass. In the afternoon the band would play in the camp for a couple of hours, and all parents and friends, and particularly the young girls, would come to hear it. It should be stressed that the Militia could be called out at any time in an emergency, but the summer camp lasted but two weeks.

Rifle practice took place at Crabbé, or one of several other rifle ranges, the men getting there by bicycle or on foot.

The greatest occasion of the militiaman's year was the Grand Review, taking place on the beach in St. Aubin's Bay, near Bel Royal, the men wearing their uniform of blue trousers and red jackets. They had to march in front of the Lieutenant-Governor, the St. Ouen's Company leading (an ancient and jealously-guarded privilege) and the Governor would deliver an oration of encouragement and praise. One hears stories of men collapsing on the sand from heat and fatigue. The review was always held on the Queen's birthday, 24 May.

In 1914, at the outbreak of war, the Militia was called up, and their duties included night watch on all the coasts. By undertaking this task they relieved the British forces of the necessity of sending troops over to do so. In March 1915, the Jersey Overseas Contingent, entirely voluntary, left Jersey. In the course of the First World War 6,292 Jerseymen served, 862 being killed, and 212 gained decorations. The Islanders were not like raw recruits, having some military experience and knowledge of handling firearms. It was a sad day for many Jerseymen when the Militia was finally disbanded in 1946, but it can look back on a long and most honourable record.

Since the 18th century regular troops have also been stationed in the Island, and this continued until 1924. It was a popular station for an infantry battalion, and all ranks enjoyed their sojourn here, and many a soldier married a local girl. At first they were stationed at Elizabeth Castle and Fort Regent, and later St. Peter's Barracks were built. These barracks were damaged during the German Occupation, and finally demolished as the airport engulfed the land in that area, after a useful life of about 140 years.

Two portraits of typical military men, taken in about 1860, are shown. One is Colonel Bauche, a Jerseyman, and the other has a notable array of medals. He is Lieutenant-Colonel J. Mauleverer, C.B., wearing the uniform of the 30th Foot, the 1st Battalion East Lancashire Regiment, stationed in Jersey in 1860. His medals, reading left to right, are: Turkish Crimea Medal; Crimea, 1854-56, with three bars; Ghuznee Medal, 1839; Order of Medjidieh, fourth class; Companion of the Bath; Sardinian War Medal; Officer of the Order of the Legion of Honour.

41.   A drill shed at St. Saviour. Of twelve drill sheds built (one for each parish) this is perhaps the only surviving photograph. It cost £2,400 to build the twelve.

42.   Rosel barracks (now a hotel). This was built in about 1810, and accommodated 68 men.

43. The Royal Naval Training School (ship) at Gorey, which existed from 1860-75, and was situated on high ground above Gorey harbour. The building behind is Old Cadet House.

44. An annual OTC inspection in 1914, at Victoria College. The Headmaster, Mr. A. H. Worrall, is seen behind Colonel Gloster, of the 1st Devonshire Regiment, the Inspecting Officer.

45. No. 1. F. Company, West Regiment of militia. 1898

46. No. 3. C. Company, East Regiment.

47.   Farmers, who were the militiamen, providing their own horses for artillery exercises. *c.* 1910.

48.   Two typical military portraits, of about 1860.
Colonel Mauleverer and Colonel Bauche.

49. No. 3. East Battalion, at a Grand Review in St. Aubin's Bay.

50. Two artillery sergeants setting out for militia duties in about 1900. They are John Ernest and Walter Philip Mourant, photographed at their home Croix ès Mottes, Maufant.

51. Built in about 1870, Beauport Battery boasted 24 pounder Bloomfield pattern guns on 1840 type carriages.

52. C. Company. Artillery, at La Collette, with 5" breech loading howitzers, in 1905.

53. A review of the garriso

tationed at Fort Regent. *c.* 1910.

54.   A group of militia cyclists, *c.* 1880.

55.   Royal Jersey Artillery, D. Company at Fort Regent, in 1907.

56. Militia artillerymen in 1900. This photograph was made into a post card, and the sender has written *"Tchi bian soudards"* (what fine soldiers).

57. The wedding of a Jersey girl to a sergeant of the
1st Devonshire Regimental Band. Between 1911-1914.

58. The departure of the Jersey Overseas Contingent. March 2nd 1915.

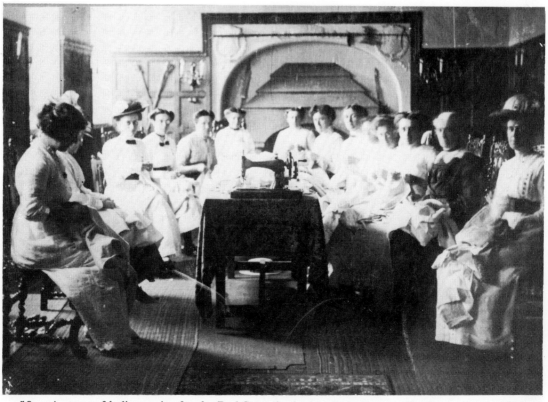

59. A group of ladies sewing for the Red Cross, in the big dining room at La Houge Boete. 1915.

PART III — SOCIAL AND COMMUNAL ACTIVITIES

During the period covered by these photographs Jersey moved forward in development, and became a society comparable to any provincial town of similar size, even if remaining slightly old-fashioned. Building raced ahead, roads were made, schools started and the harbours built or enlarged, and communications established by sea and telegraph, and various cultural and sporting societies were formed.

Life seems to have been very pleasant and enjoyable, and Mr. Le Feuvre, some of whose reminiscences have already been quoted, feels that all sections of the community were more contended than they are now, in spite of a far simpler standard of living, and regardless of whether one was rich or poor.

La Société Jersiaise was founded in 1873 as a local research and preservation society, and in the early years of this century important archaeological excavations were carried out, including work on the now world-famous palaeolithic cave at La Cotte. As this book has been compiled by La Société Jersiaise, and the photographs mainly drawn from its collections, one picture is given showing a group of its early workers, to whom we of this generation are so deeply grateful.

Through the centuries the only schools in Jersey had been St. Anastase in St. Peter, and St. Mannelier in St. Saviour, but the 19th century saw schools appearing everywhere in town and country. Victoria College was founded in 1852, and the Girls' College, then the Jersey Ladies' College, in 1880. Oxenford House in St. Lawrence was another, among many. Small 'Dame's' schools existed also, for younger children and for girls, and a group of the mistress and her pupils, of a typical example, is shown.

Bicycling became the most popular outdoor leisure activity, while horse-drawn carriages could be hired for outings and picnics, the latter being most popular, and including some rather demure rock-climbing. One of the firms running such excursions (*see* Illustration 131) was Downs of 25 David Place. They had waggonettes which called at hotels to take passengers on day or half-day excursions, and ran a double-decker horse bus, hourly, from Queen's Road to the Dicq. The picture of a King's birthday levée at Government House shows the elegance, serenity and leisure of a society which never dreamed it was on the brink of a cataclysm, with the ladies in flowing skirts and huge hats, and many of the men in uniform.

At the same time sea bathing was becoming very popular, but in a cautious and discreet manner, with bathing machines hired for undressing.

Diaries and letters of the period show what great distances people walked, both for duty and for pleasure. A letter from Sidney James Nicolle to his mother, written in 1869 says, 'I had a glorious dip this morning; I go down every morning at 7 to swim and enjoy it very much. It is very lively on the rocks at that time, bathers of all ages and descriptions, and no end of dogs'. The same writer tells us of picnics: 'Tuesday 1st September was the Joint Stock (Bank) picnic got up by Joe Dickson, the de Quettevilles etc. . . . we started . . . in two vehicles, a barouche containing Annie de Q and others, Nicolson on the box and Jack Dickson and I in the rumble. The rest of the party followed in a large waggonette. We had dinner in the usual uncomfortable style *on the grass,* and being distracted by the alternative of kneeling in a currant tart and sitting on a furze bush . . . my enjoyment . . . was not of a vivid description . . . Claret cup of a filthy taste was manufactured . . . After dinner it was resolved to visit some caves in the neighbourhood . . . but I was much relieved to hear Mary Dickson say that she could not do it, and I at once . . . offered to sit with her . . . On their return we harnessed the horses again and after a lovely moonlight drive . . . we arrived in safety . . . when we had a few dances, and home at about 12'. A few weeks later he attended another picnic 'at La Rocque or Plemont I forget which . . . I was one of a party of 15 in a three horse waggonette . . . a scramble on the rocks, when Miss Lambert and I found ourselves in an isolated position and watched porpoises in the bay and did other romantic things . . . then a dance at the hotel . . . then a drive home, coffee and more dancing then champagne, and so to bed'. Another picnic the following year was well supplied as he says, 'I shall take 36 bottles of champagne; there are to be 40 people (3 chaperones). We go out to L'Etacq in three large wagonettes'. One suspects that 'picnic' could merely mean an outing into the country. Sidney Nicolle, the very first boy to appear in the Victoria College Register, thoroughly enjoyed his return visits to his native isle after he grew up, and his relations invited him to an endless round of festivities.

Famous people visited or sojourned in the Island at all times. One of the most famous was Victor Hugo, then a political refugee, who lived here from 1853-55. His expulsion was the result of his support of the paper *L'Homme,* which published an article strongly criticising Queen Victoria. He moved on to Guernsey where he stayed for 15 years, but he re-visited Jersey on occasions.

The most dazzling local personality of the time was Lillie Langtry, née Le Breton, daughter of the Dean of Jersey. She was the friend of royalty, an actress and a racehorse owner, but she will live for ever as the epitome of beauty, widely acclaimed, and painted by several of the premier artists of the period.

60.   The party working on the excavation at the palaeolithic cave La Cotte, at St. Brelade, 1910. Left to right: G. F. B. de Gruchy, —?—, E. Daghorn, —?—, —?—, H. J. Baal, R. R. Marett, E. T. Nicolle, J. Sinel.

61.   Mr. J. Sinel working on a neolithic site at La Motte, the skull being shown in situ. October 16th, 1911.

62.　A Société Jersiaise excursion to Trinity Manor, then in a neglected state,
September 1906. **Back Row**: R. R. Lemprière, S. J. Nicolle, J. L'Amy, C.Berteau,
Rev. J. A. Balleine, A. Curry, P. A. Roissier, Rev. G. P. Balleine. **Middle Row**:
A. N. Godfray, A. H. Barreau, J. Gaudin, P. A. Aubin, Rev. F. de Gruchy.

46

F. J. Bois, Rev. E. Luce, Madame Messervy, E. C. Malet de Carteret, J. F. Giffard,
C. B. Messervy, P. Le Maistre, H. T. Bosdet, J. J. Payn, P. de C. Le Cornu,
F. P. Esnouf, Rev. J. A. Messervy, Capt. Renouf, T. Binet. **Front Row**: J. Le Bas,
E. Voisin, C. G. Le Bas, G. Vibert, H. du Parcq, E. T. Nicolle, J. A. Blampied,
C. S. Renouf.

63. An official visit to the Ecréhous, June 28th 1893. The group includes Major General Markham, the Lieutenant-Governor, Sir George Bertram, the Bailiff and Jurats.

64. The Prix d'Excellence at the Battle of Flowers in 1911. The subject was Dick Whittington, and the children shown are the late Mr. E. C. Boielle and his brother and sister. This annual festival was started in 1902, the floats gradually becoming more and more elaborate and sophisticated.

65. Laying the foundation stone of the Hermitage Breakwater, August 29th 1872, by the Bailiff, Jean Hammond.

66. A parish municipal group. The parochial officials of St. Mary, at Bel Air the home of the Constable. Between 1888-94. Amongst those shown are: **Back Row** Hotton, Reggie Arthur, Le Rossignol (Woodlands), Syvret (Le Carrefour), Le Feuvre, Jean Collas (La Frontière), Albert Arthur (Les Colombiers). **Middle Row** Le Boutillier (Haut des Buttes), Alexandre, J. S. Le Boutillier (Beechwood), Agnes (Chestnut Farm), P. J. Huelin, Constable (Bel Air), Jean Huelin (Westview), Jean Arthur (L'Ancienneté), George Dumaresq, Esnouf. **Front Row** Philip Hotton, Jean Le C. Arthur, J. S. Arthur. (We apologise to those gentlemen whose initials we have been unable to identify.)

67.   A typical Dame's school, kept by Miss Laffoley, who is shown here outside her school, now the Post Office at St. John, 1883.

68.   A common room at the Jersey Ladies' College, showing a music lesson in progress. *c.* 1890.

69.   The Victoria College Music class. 1863.

70.   A class room at the Jersey Ladies' College, founded in 1888.

71.   Oxenford House School, at St. Lawrence, now demolished. It was founded by P. Neel and J. W. E. Davey in 1870. This group was taken in 1900. Note the universal use of lace curtains, as well as blinds and shutters.

72.   A little girl, Anna Dutot, and her doll's pram with Winter Dutot, her brother (right), in about 1910.

73.   Reverend George Poingdestre, the last Regent of St. Anastase's School, St. Peter. *c.* 1860.

74. The Jersey Drag Hunt, founded before 1886, meeting at St. Peter's Barracks. The barracks were built in 1811, on a 24 acre site, purchased for £2,000.

75. The Jersey Drag Hunt meet at Petit Ménage, St. Saviour. The little girl, mounted, is May Hibbert, daughter of Colonel G. L. Hibbert D.S.O., of the King's Own Royal Lancaster Regiment, who was renting the house at the time. Between 1908-11.

54

76.   The Jersey Cycling Club. *c.* 1880

77.   La Hougue Bie, when Prince's Tower still surmounted the mound and masked the chapels, and before the neolithic tomb had been discovered. There was a hotel and a bowling alley, and tourists and residents patronised the site, as they still do, but for different reasons. The grounds now contain one of the finest neolithic tombs in Europe, two medieval chapels, an agricultural museum, a German bunker museum, a railway carriage and many other attractions.

78.   A Levée at Government House, in 1906. Note that the third storey had not then been added to the house, which was built in about 1810, but did not become the Governor's residence until 1822.

56

79. The beach at First Tower, showing the changing huts, known as bathing machines. *c.* 1900.

80. A beach scene at West Park, 1914. Note the lady reading 'The Morning News' which ceased publication in 1950.

81. A scene at the Troglodyte Caves at Five Oaks, which ceased in about 1920. They were a great tourist attraction.

82. A picnic party going down into Grève de Lecq caves.

83. The steam fire engine, the 'Lord St. Helier' in 1906, seen here with Chief Officer H. Eady, decorated as an exhibit at the Battle of Flowers.

84. Members of the Fire Brigade in about 1913. Left to right: Chief Officer Mr. Gale, P. C. Billot, Joe Remphry, Philip Denize (Caretaker, Police station).

85.   The Jersey Fire Brigade assembled at Le Hocq, for an annual outing, in about 1880.

86.   A fire brigade group taken outside the Town Hall. Note the fire engine, which can just be seen, was kept in what is now an office, and the horses were stabled in Devonshire Place.

87. An electioneering campaign, by supporters of a member of the Rose (policital) party.

88. Maison Victor Hugo, now a hotel. From a post card of 1905, with a portrait of the poet inset. He was in Jersey from 1853-1855.

89. Dean William Corbet Le Breton, his wife, son and his only daughter Lillie, the famous beauty. Her portrait was painted by many of the great artists of the day. A picture of about 1866.

90. Lillie (Mrs. Langtry), in her part of Hester Gazebrook in the play 'An unequal match'.

91.   The Cecilian Orchestra Society in 1900, founded in 1889. The President and Conductor was Mr. C. E. R. Stevens.

92.   Jersey Suffragettes outside the Morning News office in Halkett Place.

93. The lane leading to the west door of St. Martin's church. About 1900, a scene that has not changed very much.

94. Mrs. Isobel Donovan (*née* Bailey) at the gate of St. Saviour's school. It is recorded that she always polished her boots herself before going to church. Her first husband had served in the Indian Mutiny and the Crimea, and died from injuries received there.

95. The Royal Commissioners of 1860, sent to enquire into the Civil Laws of the Island. Left to right: The Earl of Devon, Sir Richard Jebb, Sir John Awdry and Mr. Percival.

96. Philippe Pinel, nicknamed Le Roi des Ecréhous, at the age of 74, with a basket he made for Princess Beatrice in 1859.

65

97.   The fourteenth century manorial chapel, dedicated to Ste. Marie, at Rosel Manor. Mrs. W. C. Lemprière can be seen with her four daughters. *c.* 1865.

98.   Peacock Farm, Trinity, so called from the topiary in the garden. That, the monkey puzzle tree, and the twelve-paned windows have all gone, but the initialled stone under the central window remains, recording an Amy-Blampied marriage in or before 1827.

PART IV—SHIPPING AND TRANSPORT

Ship-building in Jersey has gone hand in hand with the cod-fishing industry, the two crafts arising and falling together. Jerseymen were making the trans-Atlantic crossing, apparently in their own vessels, at the end of the 16th century, and continued to do so for 300 years. But it was not until about 1820 that permanent shipyards were established, starting with that of Deslandes at First Tower. By 1860 there were 18 yards round the south coast and at Gorey. There were also 'rope walks' for making the ropes and sail-lofts for making and repairing the sails. In 1864 Le Vesconte's yard at First Tower alone had eight large vessels under construction at the same time. The collapse of the ship-building industry was sudden and drastic, caused largely by the advent of iron instead of wood for hulls, and the growing dominance of steam as opposed to sail.

St. Aubin offered some shelter to ships from about 1670, and quickly developed into the shipping and commercial port of the Island. It was not until 1841 that the foundation stone of what could properly be termed a harbour at St. Helier was laid, to be officially opened a few years later by the Queen herself when she visited Jersey. This was the Victoria Pier, to be followed a few years later by the Albert Pier. But even this new harbour had a serious drawback, in that it could not be entered when the tide was low, and this at the very zenith of the shipping industry. Various plans were considered to remedy this serious disadvantage, and the great breakwater reaching south-east from St. Helier hermitage rock at Elizabeth Castle was to have been one arm of a big harbour bounded on the east side by another at La Collette; but damage by south-west gales for three successive years resulted in the scheme being abandoned in 1876. By then the shipping and cod-fishing trades had declined so much that a harbour of larger extent was no longer needful, and since then dredging has rendered the existing harbour usable at all tides.

One of the very first steamships to arrive in Jersey was the *Ariadne*, on 29 May 1824, a brave little vessel which continued in use until 1852, though not always on the Jersey run. She was soon followed by the *Lord Beresford* (named after the then Governor). The first official mail carried by a steam vessel arrived on 7 July 1827, in the *Watersprite* from Weymouth. In 1840 Southampton became linked to London by rail, and so was a more convenient port for these islands, and a swifter route for letters. Over the years these strong fearless little vessels have continued a daily link with England for both passengers and mail; they were often delayed by bad weather or the tide, but they never failed, and they constituted a part of Island life that has gone, and they are now over-shadowed by air travel. A winter crossing in a vessel such as the *Vera* could be torture to those who are not good sailors, and the sight of the dining saloon, even in a photograph may make many islanders shudder with the memory of a hurried journey to the lower decks to lie flat on one's bunk, and long for the morning. But a calm crossing could be quite delightful, and no plane journey can give the homing passenger the thrill of anticipation that was felt as La Corbière was sighted, and then passed, as he stood on deck straining his eyes to recognise passing landmarks until Elizabeth Castle came into sight and he knew that he was home.

There was talk of establishing a railway in the Island as early as 1845, mainly in the interests of defence and the swift movement of troops. Nothing, however, came of it, nor of several subsequent schemes, until 1870, when the first railway was established from St. Helier to St. Aubin. On the inaugural day the train left St. Helier at 1 o'clock, and reached St. Aubin in nine and a half minutes. There was every manifestation of enthusiasm and civic pride, and a party of dignitaries, 180 strong, had a grand lunch at Noirmont Manor, then rented by Mr. Pickering, the railway engineer, and this entertainment lasted until 7 o'clock. The very next day a section of line at La Haule, which was raised on piles, was damaged by the high tide, but repaired in the evening. This line was extended from St. Aubin to La Corbière in 1899, and it is reported that when peace was declared after the Boer War the news was carried and spread by the guard of the train calling the glad tidings out to everyone in sight, on roads or in the fields. Soon after the Western Railway, the Jersey Eastern Company opened a line from St. Helier to Gorey, and in both cases the journey took the passengers beside the sea coast, giving panoramic views all the way.

These railways, which maintained a remarkably high degree of safety and punctuality, performed an enormous service to the Island over the 60 and more years of their existence, and they were used by all branches of the community. It was not unknown for a lady who had arrived slightly late for her train at La Haule halt, to wave her umbrella at the driver, who would stop, and reverse the train back to the platform. Before the days of private cars they (with horse-drawn buses) provided the only means of getting to such distant parts as Gorey and La Corbière, the favourite picnic spots, and to St. Brelade's Bay, although that meant a fairly long walk from Don Bridge station. The trains were much used by schoolchildren, and in the case of the western line there was the additional thrill when a high tide swept over the sea-wall at First Tower and West Park.

99. A ship building yard at First Tower—Deslandes, one of the most important. *c.* 1870.

100. Shipyards at Havre des Pas. Valpy, Vautier and Allix had yards situated here.

101. Shipyards at La Collette. Bisson's yard was situated here. Note the small, single storey, houses, no hotels and no sea wall or bathing pool.

102. Shipyard in St. Aubin's Bay.

103. Shipyards at Gorey.

104. *The Agilis of Guernsey*, in Gorey harbour.

105. St. Helier's harbour during the potato season. Note the steam cranes.

106. *HMS Dasher* in Gorey harbour. She arrived in Jersey in 1838 on mail service, later serving in the Crimea. In 1860 she returned to Jersey as a fishery protection vessel, based at Gorey. In 1884 she was replaced by *HMS Mistletoe.*

107. *S.S. Diana* leaving St. Helier's harbour. She was commissioned as a mail boat in 1876, and was wrecked off the Little Russel Passage near Guernsey in 1895, without loss of life. The lamp showing at the pierhead was re-erected at Gorey, where it remained until recently.

108. An early picture of St. Helier's harbour. Commercial Buildings 'Le Quai des Marchands' can be seen on the right.

109. *S.S. Ibex* off Elizabeth Castle. Built in 1891, this record-breaking but ill-fated vessel had an interesting career, more than once being involved in collisions. In 1900 she struck a rock off Guernsey and sank, and was not salvaged until six months later. She was broken up in 1926.

110. The dining saloon on board the *S.S. Vera*, which first came to the Channel Islands in 1898. During the first war she sank a German U-boat. The décor is typical of the period.

111. The maiden voyage of the *S.S. Roebuck*, July 1st 1897. In 1911 she struck a rock in St. Brelade's Bay. In 1915 at Scapa Flow she broke her moorings, rammed at battleship, and sank.

112. *S.S. Roebuck* precariously perched on the Kaines Rocks in St. Brelade's Bay. *c.* 1911.

113. Captain James Goodridge who died in 1876, was the famous son of a famous father, who commanded mailships of the London and South Western Railway Company.

114. Carriages meeting the *S.S. Alberta*. She was built in 1900, and was finally bombed and sunk in 1941, having passed to Greek ownership. Note coaches from the hotels meeting prospective clients, the *Star*, *Bree's Royal* and the *Royal Yacht*; and on the left is the van of W. Gray, furniture and luggage carrier.

115. Passengers on board the *S.S. Antelope*. She first came to Jersey in 1889, and was later sold to a Greek firm, and was captured in the Mediterranean in 1914.

116. Carriages on the Weighbridge area, before the statue of Queen Victoria, and the garden surrounding it, were made, and the northern part of the harbour filled in. Before 1880.

117. The same scene, in 1905, with the statue. This central area is now an assembly point for buses.

118. September 29th 1870 was the trial run f[...]
and the photograph taken on the return journe[...]
declining shipyards, Deslandes, at First Tower.

e Jersey Western Railway. The engine was the *Haro Haro*,
4.20 p.m. The open carriages were built at one of the then

119. Construction work on the railway between La Haule and St. Aubin. This shows the first railway engine to be seen in Jersey. 1870.

120. The Jersey Western Railway engine *Duke of Normandy*, one of two originals, at St. Helier's Terminus station. Fourth from the left is Mr. Squibb, the Town Station Master.

121. The railway station at Gorey village, typical of the station buildings on the Eastern railway, which were rather more substantial than those built on the Western.

122. The Terminus station at St. Aubin. It is not known for what occasion the station was so gaily decorated, but it looks as if it might have been some naval event.

123. The Jersey Eastern Railway engine *Calvados*, built in 1872 and condemned in 1927, this was perhaps the best engine ever to run on the local lines.

124. **and 125.** Other forms of transport. A two seater pony trap, in front of a thatched barn containing straw, and a lady and her young daughter in a donkey cart.

126. Mrs. Guiton, mother of Mr. Guiton, to whose memory this book is dedicated. Her son, who took the photograph on November 26th 1899, at Victoria Tower, records that he gave a 15 second exposure at 2 feet distance. Note there are no mudguards on the bicycle.

127. A tandem and trailer in 1903. The rider is Mr. Guiton.

83

128. Stated to be Frank Swan, a photographer of 29, David Place, about to go for a drive in a phaeton.

129. (*right*)   Campbell, a well known guide, who accompanied horse-drawn coach excursions, giving travellers a racy account of all they saw on their drive.

130. A picnic party outside *Rozel Bay Hotel. c. 1875.*

131. Varied forms of transport. A harbour scene in about 1910.

132. About to go visiting. Mrs. Collas, in Clarendon Road, with the pony Peggy, and the coachman Mr. T. Legg.

133. A harbour scene at the hei
The sailing ship visible on the lef
foundland trader.

the potato season, in about 1910.
e brigantine *Dawn*, a Jersey—New-

PART V — TOWN AND CRAFTS

In the course of the 19th century St. Helier rose out of its mediaeval lethargy, accepted its rôle as the social and commercial centre of the Island, and developed rapidly. We have already seen how the harbour evolved and trade routes expanded.

The Royal Square is the focal point of the town. Once the market place, it has also always contained the site of the Insular Government buildings; it is the place where Charles II was proclaimed King in 1649, when no other part of his domain accepted him, and the area where the Battle of Jersey was fought, and won, and it remains the natural rallying point on all important occasions, as was seen at the time of the Liberation. The photographs are able to show some of the houses which have quite disappeared on the south side of the square, the whole of that side now being taken up by the States and Court buildings.

The General Post Office has had six homes, before coming to its present one in Broad Street. It started in Hue Street in 1794, and we show the Headquarters it occupied in Halkett Place from 1881-1909.

A list of 24 public pumps situated in the town has been compiled. A few were on private property, but all were accessible to the public, who, until the middle of the 19th century, had no other water supply, unless fortunate enough to have wells in their own gardens. As the population increased the public supplies tended to become contaminated in crowded areas, and in 1832, and again in 1849, there was an outbreak of cholera. There was, until about 1840, no modern drainage system.

Hotels sprang up to meet the ever-increasing demands of tourists, and for townspeople it was an adventure to stay in a country hotel, or even to go there for a meal, or to hire rooms in a farm for the 'change of air' so much prescribed by doctors. At the same time the shops became more numerous, and better stocked, and the markets were improved. Moved from the Royal Square in 1800, the stallholders were provided with a fine and picturesque new market in Beresford Street. However, even that gradually became over-crowded and the present spacious and attractive one was built in 1882. There had been a separate fish market in Cattle Street, which has been only recently demolished.

In a community which depends on horse power for agriculture, transport and leisure, the smith was one of the most important members of the community, hence the preponderance of the name Smith in England,

and Le Feuvre (Latin *faber*) in Jersey. So it is appropriate that at least one forge should be shown. This smithy still operates, and is likely to continue, as the horse population of the Island again builds up to considerable numbers (it is said to be 2,000 in 1975) although hardly used in agriculture now. On the door of this forge can be seen dozens of initials, shown by the syllables of the name, as is the Jersey fashion; these show where the smith has tested brands which he has made for individual farmers to have their implements marked.

The two best known brick-making families were the Copps and the Champions, and their brick kilns used to be a familiar sight at Five Oaks and Mont à l'Abbé until recent years. In early centuries granite was the universal building material, but from about 1760 brick appeared, though not on a large scale. As the 19th century advanced more and more brick was used in the towns and suburbs, though rarely in the country.

Off the coast of Jersey there are two groups of islets, the Ecréhous to the east and the Minquiers to the south. Early photographers do not appear to have taken their cameras on their fishing expeditions, and so records are scarce. These islands were the subject of a case between France and England at the International Court of Justice at The Hague in 1953, when Jersey's claim to them was upheld. They are natural sanctuaries for wild life, particularly birds, and a great source of shell fish.

In conclusion it can be said that this is a vanishing Jersey which has been shown to you; people, scenes, buildings and activities that many readers will recall, an Island in some ways less comfortable and agreeable than it now is, but in many ways recording a life regretted by those who knew it, and perhaps coveted by those who did not.

BEAUMONT, JERSEY, WESTERLY VIEW.

134. A scene which, apart from the traffic, has not changed greatly. Beaumont village. *c.* 1895.

135. Morier Lane, now the upper part of Halkett Place. In the middle distance is the eastern end of the Court and States buildings, completed between 1866-96. In the distance is Fort Regent.

136. The south side of the Royal Square, before the present States' buildings were erected. St. Helier's church is in the background, and on the right the building which was Le Halle à Blé (Cornmarket) when the square was the market place. The square was paved in 1818.

137. The Royal Square. The chestnut trees, planted in 1894, are quite young, and a farmer takes his load of empty potato barrels up a road now choked with cars. In the middle background is the *Peirson Hotel*, so called after the hero of the Battle of Jersey, who was mortally wounded near there in 1781.

138. Elizabeth Castle, showing St. Helier's Hermitage, when the breakwater was about to be built, 1872. Note the railway lines for transport of materials, and the lone horse.

139. The Post Office, now the Mechanics Institute, in Halkett Place. This building was in use as a Post Office from 1881-1909.

140. Beresford Street, with a cab rank on the right. The cabs are ranged in front of the market, built in 1882.

141. Hill Street, with the back of the Royal Court Building, in 1880. This shows one of the town pumps, known as La Pompe des Gens de Droit, so called as most of the lawyers had, and still have, their offices in Hill Street.

142. King Street, showing cobble stones. Now that this road is a pedestrian precinct it is regaining something of the leisurely character shown in this photograph of about 1910.

143. *The Marine Hotel*, previously called
present *Grand Hotel* is on the same site,

the *Hotel Empress Eugénie*, in about 1870. The
though built further back from the road.

144. *The Terminus Hotel* at St. Aubin, with a party of excursionists preparing to set out, drawn by four horses. This building later became the railway terminus, and is now the offices of the Constable of St. Brelade.

145. *The Royal Yacht Hotel* in Caledonia Place, to which two extra storeys were added later. The delicate awnings and wrought iron work of the balconies have quite disappeared.

146. *Prince's Hotel* at Havre des Pas, evidently much patronised by the soldiery, stationed at Fort Regent.

147. A scene outside Orviss' in Beresford Street, in about 1914. The prices should be noticed.

148. (*left*) A tobacconist's shop in King Street, now the *Maison Kerdal.*

149. A posed photograph at Le Quesne's the wine merchants. *c.* 1912.

150. (*left*)   The Beresford Library, kept by
C. Le Feuvre, a printer who did most excellent
work. Note the firm's delivery cart. 1894.

151. (*below*)   Inside the library. The librarian is
Mr. Sweeney, and writing at a desk is Mr. du Parcq,
who afterwards opened a bookshop in Halkett
Place, and was the father of Lord du Parcq.

152. (*above*) The market, built in 1882, shown in about 1907. Note the gas lighting. The main structure and central fountain have not changed.

153. (*left*) The Fish market, built in 1841, now demolished. Note the predominance of conger eels among the fish shown.

154. Mr. Bouchéré's cart, delivering goods, with its well-known symbol of La Corbière lighthouse at the back. 1915.

155. Mr. Oldridge's meat delivery van. *c.* 1900.

156. de Faye's shop in David Place, with their delivery van. *c.* 1900.

157. de Faye's bottling plant, for mineral waters.

158. Men working at Vatcher's China clay Quarries at Handois in 1906. The horse, named Prince, is held by Elie Le Brun and others in the group include John Edward Gavey, Fred and John Collas, and Tom Dwyer.

159. Again at the Quarries, with a horse named Lisette, held by Edouard John Gavey, with Philip Collas to the right. The cart would make two journeys daily to town, to take the loads of china clay to commercial buildings, for export to England. Mr. Gavey was paid 15/- per week. The quality of these two photographs is due to them having been rescued from an attic, the only records of these quarries found.

160. A view of Copp's Brickfields at Five Oaks. There are no kilns surviving now.

161. A group of workers at the brickfield in 1889. The kiln shown was called the Great Eastern. The workers are, **left to right:** Jules Le Becher, Alfred Le Conte, Frank Le Conte, William Hutchings, Harris, ?, George Le Conte, Harry Turner, George Hutchings, Joe Morcel, Harry Harris, Fred Taisnel, Charles Copp, George Copp, George Hutchings (? jnr.), Celestin Dorleans, Frank David, Mrs. George Hutchings, who has brought some refreshments. George Le Conte was a champion brickmaker, and could make twelve bricks during the time it took the church clock to strike 12. He was paid 3/4d per thousand. During bad weather the clay could not be prepared, and wages were poor. The work caused the men's hands to become sore with deep chaps, which they sealed with shoemaker's wax softened over a candle.

162. (*above*) The forge on the road from St. Martin's church to Rosel. The smith was Mr. Robins, who was a farrier, wheelwright and also made ploughs and other farm implements. Mr. P. Jehan's horse is being shod.

163. (*left*) Jimmy Walker, a scissor grinder, of Pier Road. *c.* 1900.

164. At Jerrom's rope walk at Havre des Pas. The photograph shows Mr. Jerrom and his son with combed hemp, ready to wind ropes. It was taken in about 1920, but shows probably the last workers of this most ancient craft.

165. Kite flying was a popular sport at this period. *c.* 1912.

166. Fishermen at Les Ecréhous. Note the man on the right holding a conger eel, and in addition to lobster pots, there is a shrimping net and a sand eel basket. To the right can be seen a tree mallow plant, a species which grows freely on these rocky islets. 1883.

167. Shrimping at Les Minquiers, the group of islets to the south.

168. West Park, a scene that has changed considerably. Note the military picket house, in use when a detachment of the garrison was at Elizabeth Castle, the now vanished railway line, and a row of bathing machines. Now there is a German bunker at the corner.

169. Portrait of Miss Neel. *c.* 1860.

170. Portrait of an unknown girl. *c.* 1860.

171. A corner near St. John's Church, which has changed considerably, *c.* 1895.

172. Portrait of Charles Henry Poingdestre, 1892-1905, President of the British Academy in Rome.

173. A family group. *c.* 1860.

174. (*above*) Sir Robert Pipon Marett, Bailiff, 1820-84, as a young man. This is the only daguerrotype found where the sitter could be identified with certainty, and it was taken by Mullins of the Royal Square, in about 1850.

175. (*right*) An advertisement for a very early photographer. This notice appeared in the local press in September 1843. *Lozey's Hotel* was at the Weighbridge.

PHOTOGRAPHIC PORTRAITS.

MR. A. BARBER, Proprietor of the Photographic Institution, Nottingham, and late Operator at the Royal Polytechnic Institution, London, begs to inform the Nobility, Gentry, Visitors, and Inhabitants of Jersey, that in consequence of the numerous solicitations to visit the island, he is now having erected at considerable expense a suitable *Operating Room* on the leads of Lozey's Hôtel de Paris, Pier, commanding splendid light, and affording every facility for obtaining the finest effects of light and shade in taking Photographic Portraits. The peculiar feature in Mr. Barber's process is one of paramount importance in a Portrait, *they are not reversed*, which is the case by all other methods, thereby giving a likeness of extraordinary fidelity surpassing the most exquisite work of the human hand.

Mr. Barber takes this opportunity of stating that the apparatus used by him, and the process altogether, is precisely the same as Mr. Beard's, at the Polytechnic Institution, London, he having purchased the right of using the patent.

The eminent success which has attended Mr. Barber's practise of the Art at Guernesey, is a sufficient proof of the high estimation in which his Portraits are held, having been honoured by the patronage of some of the first families in that Island.

N. B.—The clear shining of the sun is *not necessary* to the success of the operation, many of the finest specimens having been taken in cloudy weather.

Specimens may be seen at Lozey's Hotel, Messrs Sullivan's, Halkett-place, " British Press" office, and " Chronique" office.

☞ The day of opening will be announced in next week's paper.

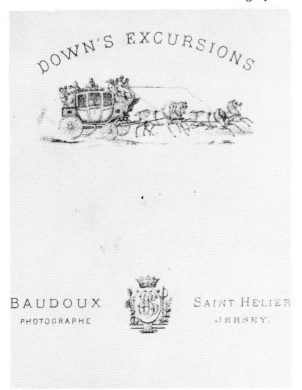

176. Baudoux and Sons, also advertising Down's excursions.

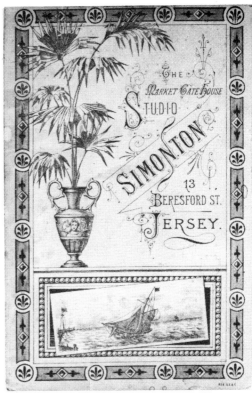

177. Simonton, 13, Beresford Street. (1885-1898).

178. C. Ouless, 53, New Street. (1871-1914).

179. Baudoux, 59, New Street. (1869-1894).

ALPHABETICAL LIST OF PHOTOGRAPHERS ACTIVE IN JERSEY BETWEEN 1842-1918

Name	Address	In operation
American Portrait Art Co.	21 Broad Street	1909
Anthoine, Mrs.	34 Aquila Road	1862-65
Asplet & Green	18½ Beresford Street	1866-75
Aubin & Murrow	Colomberie	1893
Barber, A., Itinerant	Roof of *Lozey's Hotel*	1843, Sept.
Bashford, George	15 Bath Street	1859-62
Bashford, James	12 Bath Street	1859-62
Bashford & Mercier	15 Bath Street	1867-71
Barnard, E.	1 Peirson Place	1881
Baudoux, E. & Sons	59 New Street; 11 Craig Street	1869-94
„ „ „	51½ and 56 New Street	Sold to Albert Smith
Bennetts, C.	15 Queen Street	*c.* 1890
Bensa, G.	6 Old Street	1869
Berger, H.	4 David Place	1866
Berger & Asplet	20½ Beresford Street	1864-65
Bettell, C.	?	*c.* 1890
Billinghurst & Downham	16 Royal Parade	?
Billinghurst & Smith	13 and 16 Parade	1885-93
Billinghurst, F. H.		1893
Bouillards, Daguerrotype Photographers	16 Mulcaster Street	*c.* 1850
Burman, F.	4 David Place	1867-71
Clarke, A. H.	1 Queen Street	1910
Clarke, F. W.	27 Halkett Place	1909
Collie, J.	2 Belmont Road	1861-64
Collie, William	2 Belmont Road	pre 1850–72
Cook, W.	Parade	1859
Daly, D.	Colomberie	1869
Daly, J.	5 La Motte Street; 23 Colomberie; 6 Francis Street	1872-80
Daly, J.	1 Bellozanne Road	1907-09
Davey, W. T.	6 Charing Cross; 15 Queen Street	1859-76

Name	Address	In operation
Deane, F. D.	26 Bath Street	1866
de Beer, Cecil	17 and 27 Halkett Place ..	1905-08
de Beer & Lloyd	27 Halkett Place	1906
Delatour, M.	28 David Place	1850-66
Dovey, W. J., Vandyke Studio	16 Royal Parade	1901-11
Dubreuil, P.	2 Peter and 52 New Street ..	1865-77
Duguey, E., New Town Studio	David Place	1909-11
Dumaresq R. (Group and Landscape photographer) ..	13 Parade	?
Dunham, Percival	57 Bath Street	1911-14
Dunn, H.	23 Colomberie	1862-65
Eager, Robert	57 Bath Street	1873-1905
Etasse, H., Jersey Photographic Artist	?	c. 1890
Eureka Photographic Co. ..	1 New Town Buildings, David Place	1899-1903
Foot, F.	6 Pitt Street	1914
Gee, C. E. P., American Studio	4 Peter Street; 4 David Place ..	1871-90
Gee, Palmer	4 Peter Street, Morier Lane and Bath Street	1859-75
Godfray, P.	Royal Square, 61 New Street; 16 Bath Street; 35 Belmont Road	1859-1900
Godfray, H. S.	11 Library Place	1901
Green, John	18½ Beresford Street	1876-82
Gregory & Eddy	15 Bath Street amd 28 Halkett Place	1871-72
Gregory, W. W.	15 Bath Street	1867-78
Greatorex, G.	4 David Place	1867
Guillon, V.	61 New Street	1880
Halkett Studio	27 Halkett Place	1910
Hazart, C.	45 Bath Street	1880-83
Hopkins, E.	16 Parade	1913
Hutton, F. B.	74 St. John's Road	1882
Jaquiery, J.	Eton Lodge, Don Road ..	1880
Johnson, T.	58 King Street	1886
Jones, W. & Co.	13 Beresford Street, 'Market Gate House'	1871-75

Name	Address	In operation
Katz, D.	26 Union Street	1901
Kilner, Francis G.	12 Grenville Street and 34 Aquila Road	1859-66
„ „	Mont Félard Cottage, Millbrook	Returned 1873
Kinght, W. S. & T. S., Sussex Photographic Co.	5 Cheapside; 15 Parade ..	1880-85
Koeppen, A.	Don View Studio, 36 Parade ..	1892
Lacolley, J.	45 Bath Street	1876-77
Langlois, G.	12 Bath Street	1867-71
La Sauce, Adolphe	34 New Street and 5 La Motte Street	1872-80
Laurens, A.	6 York Street	1899–.....
Le Cordier, L.	22 David Place	1883
Le Sueur, F.	16 Royal Parade	1859-69
Le Sueur Ph.	16 Royal Parade	1882
London Carbon Photographic Co.	15 Parade	1884
Maguire, Julian B.	1 New Town Buildings, David P. Electric Light Studio ..	1881-99
Marius, M.	2 David Place	1876-79
Maubant	St. Mark's Road	1859
Mévius fils.	9 David Place	1889-90
Miraldi, W.	42 King Street	1911
Moore, Ellis	Bath Street	
Moore, T. H.	Bath Street	1865-66
Mullins, Henry	Royal Saloon, 7 Royal Square	1849-73
Myers	St. Saviour's Road	1859
Mercier, F. H.	5 Belmont Road	1872
McKeown, T.	5 La Motte Street	1885-90
Ogier, E.	45 Bath Street	1874-76
Ouless, C. P.	46-48 New Street and 53 New Street	1871-1914
Picot, Joshua	11 Beresford Street	1859-69
Poore, P.	6 Francis Street	?
Price, T. & Son	2, 3, 4 Peter Street; 15 Queen Street	1869-1914
Roemhild, Monsieur (Itinerant)	At the house of Madame Date, 'Laura Cottage', St. Saviour's Road	1842

Name	Address	In operation
Rosière, J. C.	2 Francis Street	1862
Seeney, C.	6 Hilary Street and 26 Queen Street	1867-73
Sharp, W. L.	2 David Place and 1 Peirson Place	1869-73
Simonton, J., Jr.	45 Bath Street	1885
Simonton Bros.	13 Beresford Street and 45 Bath Street	1889-98
Sinel, A. G.	61 New Street	1861
Smith, Albert (Ltd.)	13 Beresford Street; 45 Bath Street; 3 Broad Street ..	1894–.....
Spencer, H.	5 La Motte Street .. :.	1883
Stewart Villiers, H.	45 Bath Street	1885
Stroud, J. R. G.	59 New Street	1888-90
Swan, Frank B.	28 David Place and Langley House, St. Saviour	1868-77
Taylor, T., American Gem Photographer	4 Peter Street	*c.* 1890
Tibbles, T.	5 King Street and 1 Peirson Place	1876-77
Toovey & Snow	36 Royal Parade	1894
Toovey, E. Hamilton	36 Royal Parade	1895-1913
Tynan Bros.	41 Bath Street	1886–.....
Vandycke, V. E.	16 Parade	1894-1900
Wadsworth	Ann Street	1859

(The above details are taken mainly from the trade directories, beginning in the 1850s, in the 'Almanacs of Jersey'. Dates after 1918, the range of this book, have not been given.)

THE TOWN OF St HELIER, JERSEY

showing the location of photographs appearing
in this book